PERFECT
PAPERCRAFT

Cards
and Gifts

P E R F E C T
PAPERCRAFT

Cards and Gifts

[OVER 20 beautiful paper projects to make GIFTS, CARDS & DECORATIONS]

PaRragon

Bath · New York · Singapore · Hong Kong · Cologne · Delhi
Melbourne · Amsterdam · Johannesburg · Auckland · Shenzhen

First published by Parragon in 2012

Parragon
Queen Street House
4 Queen Street
Bath BA1 1HE, UK
www.parragon.com

Designed by Pink Creative Ltd
Projects designed by Geff Newland

ISBN 978-1-4454-7295-9
Printed in China

Introduction

Perfect Papercraft Cards and Gifts gives you all you need to create more than 20 beautiful projects that are ideal for birthdays and gifts to give to your closest friends and family for every occasion throughout the year. Follow the simple instructions and you'll be able to make all of these stunning items with a minimum of stress. We've printed and punched the templates for each project so all you need to do is push them out and follow the easy step-by-step instructions. The only equipment you need is adhesive, such as PVA, and some ribbon for the fancy boxes.

Each project has been given a star rating, from one to five, to show you how difficult it is to make - from the simplest napkin rings to the more complex New Home Card. Don't worry, even if you've not done a lot of craft before, you'll soon be making the more tricky gifts with ease.

The book is divided into different gift ideas covering everything from greeting cards for every occasion and ornaments so good you'll want to keep them yourself, to divine photo frames and gorgeous gift boxes. The final chapter gives you everything you will need to celebrate in style with bunting and place settings for your party guests. What are you waiting for? Dive in!

Greeting Cards

Materials	Skill Level
Card pattern from page 73 Glue, 1 x C5 Envelope (229x162mm/9x6in)	

Attach the front to the base

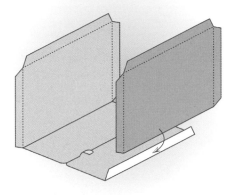

1 } Pre-crease all folds before gluing anything together. Glue the front of the house to the base piece, attaching the glue flap to the white locating panel.

Fold the sides

2 } Fold one of the sides in half, so the two white panels meet, and glue together. Repeat for the other end piece.

Glue on the ends

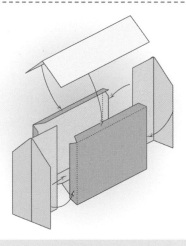

3 } Glue the two ends to the house sides. This is easier if the house is flat on a table. Attach the roof, making sure the glue tabs on the house are perfectly lined up with the white locating panels on the roof. To 'pop' the house, push the ends of the house together until they 'click' into place.

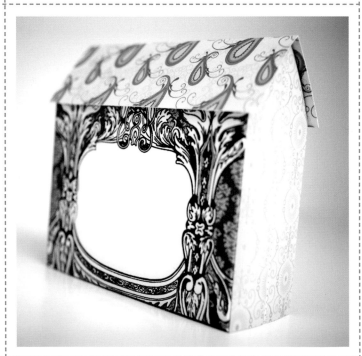

New Home Card

This gorgeous card is the perfect way to wish a friend or loved one lots of happiness in their new home.

Happy Returns Hen

A one-off quirky and jolly creation to give to a special friend on their birthday.

Tweet! Tweet!

Form the body

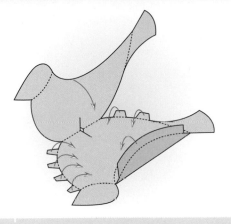

1 } Pre-crease all folds before gluing anything together. Lay the body down on a table with the patterned side face down. Fold over all the little glue flaps and the long flap across the hen's back. Put a small amount of glue on all the flaps and fold over the body. Press down until the glue sets.

Add the wing

2 } Using a small dot of glue, attach the wing to the side of the body. Don't glue the whole of the wing, just an area the size of the grey dot. This will enable the wing to kick out from the body slightly.

Pop into shape

3 } Only pop the hen into shape if you are keeping her for yourself, otherwise you may damage the body when you come to flatten it. To pop her into shape, hold the body in one hand and gently push the dot with a finger. Use the stand to allow the hen to stay upright.

Materials	Skill Level
Card pattern from page 79 Glue, 1 x C6 Envelope (162x114mm/6x4.5in)	

Fold the cake

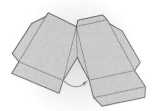

1} Pre-crease all folds before gluing anything together. Lay the cake with the icing side face down. Now fold the cake to create an upside-down 'V', but don't glue it!

Glue flaps

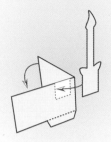

2} Fold the cake in half and glue the two glue flaps to the white locating panels.

Attach a candle

3} Fold the candle stand in half and glue together. Glue the candle to the candle stand at the position shown.

Add the gift tag

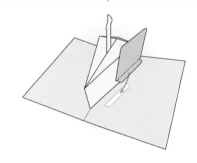

7} Leave the glue to set and then slowly and carefully open the card. If this is done before the glue has set, the cake will pull away from the card. Finally, glue the gift tag to the card.

Happy Birthday Card

This delicious birthday cake card looks good enough to eat!

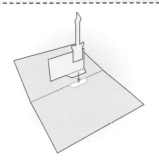

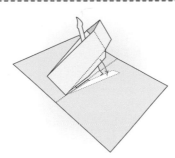

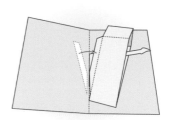

4 } Next, glue the candle stand onto the card at tho place shown. Make sure the stand sits exactly on the crease line and not to one side.

5 } Carefully slide the cake over the candle and glue the right-hand glue flap onto the card at the position shown.

6 } Lay the cake down flat to the right-hand side. Apply some glue to the glue flap on the cake, then close the card and press down firmly until the glue sets.

Sweet Treat!

Let it
Snow!

Snowflake Greeting Card

Make this Christmas card with a classic snowflake design for a
lucky friend.

Attach the thread

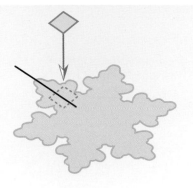

1 } Cut a 4cm (1.5in) length of white cotton thread. Using a small piece of sticky tape, stick the thread to the back of one of the snowflakes, allowing no more than 1.5mm (0in) to extend from the snowflake.

Glue together

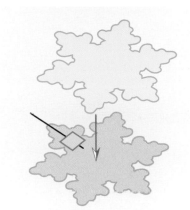

2 } Glue the two snowflakes together, back to back.

Finish assembling

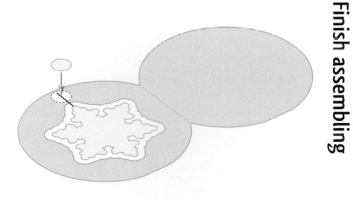

3 } Place the open card on a flat surface and lay the snowflake in the hole in the card. Glue the disk over the thread making sure it the glue has dried before closing the card.

Card pattern from page 85
1 x C6 Envelope (162x114mm/6x4.5in)
Double sided sticky foam pads, Scissors

Make a 3-D effect

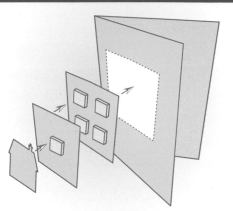

1} Pre-crease all folds before gluing anything together. Start on the front of the card by gluing the background layer 1 to the white area. Now take a sticky pad and cut it into four. Apply the four small pads to the background layer 1. Remove the backing paper from the pads and stick background layer 2 to them. Finally, using 1 whole pad, apply the mini house as the top layer giving a 3-D relief effect to the front of the card.

Attach the house

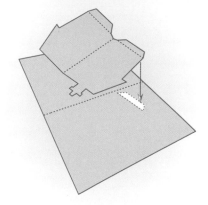

2} Open up the card and lay it on a flat surface. Take the house piece and glue the right hand glue flap to the right hand glue area of the card.

Glue and fold the house

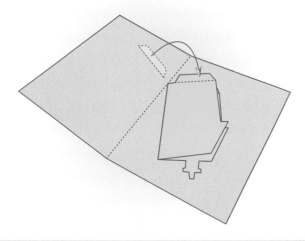

3} Now fold the house piece in half and apply glue to the last glue flap. Then fold the card in half and press firmly on the area of the glue flap. Make sure the glue has set before opening the card.

Add the heart

4} We have also supplied a heart shape, which you can use to make your own pop-up card. Use the same technique as described in steps 2 to 3 to attach the heart to the inside of your card.

Pop-up House Card

This 3-D card is very easy to make but the results are simply stunning, and will really make it stand out from the crowd.

There's no place like Home!

Materials	Skill Level
Card pattern from page 89 Glue, 1 x C5 Envelope (229x162mm/9x6in) Sticky tape, Cotton thread, Scissors, Ruler	

Pop-up Tea Cup

Take a break with this delicate cup and saucer. This won't look out of place on any well-laid table.

Add the supports

1\} Pre-crease all folds before gluing anything together. Lay the cup on a flat surface with the pattern face down. Take one of the two supports and fold it into a 'W' shape. Glue one end of the support to the white position mark on the cup, making sure it is facing the correct way as shown in the drawing. Repeat for the other support. Then fold the cup in half and glue the tab to the white position mark.

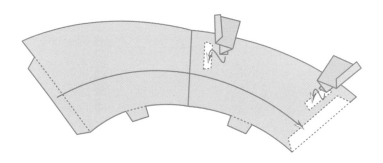

Stick on the tag

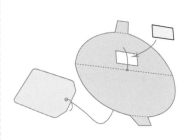

2\} Cut a 15cm (6in) length of the cotton and push one end through the hole in the centre of the tea piece. Secure the end with a small piece of sticky tape. Tie the other end to the tag.

Add the tea

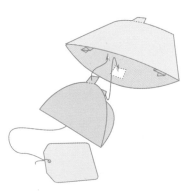

3\} Fold the tea piece in half and glue the two glue tabs to the white position marks inside the cup. Make sure when you do this that the tea piece is parallel to the top of the cup – *see* the picture in Step 4.

Attach the saucer

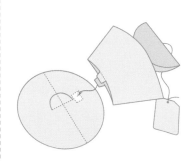

4\} Lay the saucer on a flat surface and then glue one of the tabs on the bottom of the cup onto the white position mark on the saucer.

Tea Party!

Add the handles

5 } Put a small amount of glue on the remaining tab on the cup and then fold the saucer in half. Press down firmly around the glue tab area, waiting until the glue has set before opening up the saucer. Take the two halves of the handle and glue them back-to-back, then glue it to the cup at the position marked on the cup.

Open up and glue on the teaspoon

6 } To finish, carefully open up the saucer and push the tea part down until it 'pops' into place. Glue the teaspoon onto the saucer, taking care not to glue it across the crease in the saucer or you could prevent the card from folding flat. To close, gently pull the tag upwards and the cup will start to collapse.

Ornaments

Je t'aime!

Origami Heart

Simply made from one piece of paper, this heart is created using the ancient Japanese art of origami.

Materials	Skill Level

Card pattern from page 93
Glue

Fold the top point

1 } Pre-crease all folds before gluing anything together. Place the square of card on a flat surface with the plain pink side face up and with the dark pink dot at the top. Fold the top point down to the centre.

Fold the lower point

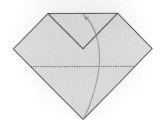

2 } Now fold the lower point up to meet the top edge.

Fold the sides

3 } Fold the two sides in at 45 degrees so they meet in the middle. Apply a small amount of glue at the two points shown in the diagram.

Flip the top point

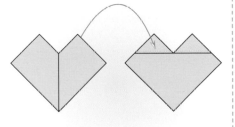

4 } Turn the heart over, taking care not to smear the glue.

Glue to complete

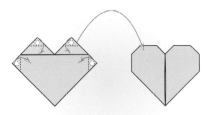

5 } Fold over the left and right corners, followed by the two top corners. Apply a small amount of glue to hold them down. Turn the heart back over to finish.

Materials		Skill Level
Card pattern from page 95 Glue		✳ ✳ ✳ ✳ ✳

Glue the struts

1} Pre-crease all folds. Glue the four struts to the four white glue positions on the Home 1 piece.

Fold and line up the struts

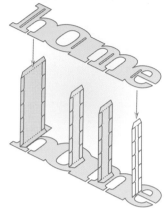

2} Fold over all of the little tabs. Then line up the struts with the slots on Home 2 and push Home 2 down until it sits on top of the bottom tabs.

Home Sweet Home!

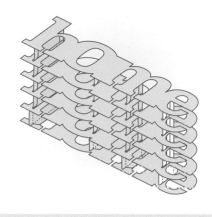

3} Do the same for Home 3.

4} Continue repeating the process for Home 4 and Home 5. Finish by gluing Home 6 to the glue tabs at the top of the struts.

Home Letters

A simple project that has a big impact, using different layers to produce a 3-D effect.

Glue the tabs

1} Pre-crease all folds before gluing anything together. Glue the five small glue tabs on one side of the top to the reverse side of the bird back. This is a bit tricky as everything is curved, but make sure each of the tabs is glued well.

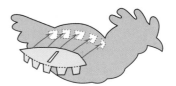

Add the head and tail

2} Glue the bird front to the five remaining tabs on the top panel. Finally, applying a little dot of glue, stick the head and tail together to create a curved body.

Make the legs

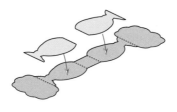

3} Place the legs on a flat surface with the patterned side facing down. Take the two inside leg panels and glue them to the legs, creating a double thickness of card.

Glue on the pivot

4} Fold the pivot in half and glue to the top of the legs. Then finish the leg piece by gluing the two bottom panels to the base. The legs will slightly angle inwards at the base.

Weight the body

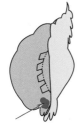

5} Take a small, pea-sized piece of tack adhesive and stick it inside the hen's body, where the tail glues together. This will act as a counter weight.

Rock the bird

6} Slot the hen's body over the pivot. The hen should balance, which will enable her to rock. If the tail is pointing upwards, you will need to add a little more tack adhesive. If her head is pointing upwards, remove a small amount of the tack adhesive until she balances and gently rocks when you tap her head.

Rocking Bird

A cute little bird decoration that rocks back and forth. Easy to make and ideal as a birthday gift.

Cluck! Cluck!

Indulge!

Cupcake

Sit back and enjoy this delicious-looking cupcake. This gift is easy to make but will be a joy to give or receive.

Materials	Skill Level
Card pattern from page 101 Glue	✱ ✱ ✱ ✱ ✱

Make the cupcake

1 } Start with the Cake Top with the patterned side face up. Carefully glue each of the little tabs to the wing next to it. As you do so, the Cake Top will start to form a dome shape. Take care not to tear the card near the centre of the dome as you bend each wing into place.

Attach the cake bottom

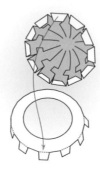

2 } Now glue the Cake Top to the Cake Bottom by lining up the tabs with the little dotted blue glue areas. Use the hole in the centre of the Cake Bottom to get your fingers inside to make sure the tabs are properly stuck down.

Curl the case

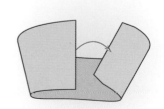

3 } Take the Case and with the spotted side up, gently curl it over the edge of a table to form a smooth curve. Try not to crease or dent the card while doing so. Glue the two ends together to form a dumpy, open-ended cone.

Attach the case

4 } Line up the tabs on the Cake Bottom to the dotted blue glue areas on the inside of the Case. Glue each of the little tabs to the Case.

Add the finishing touches

5 } To finish the cupcake, use a small dab of glue to attach the Decoration.

Materials	Skill Level

Card pattern from page 103
Glue, Ballpoint pen, Thick cotton thread,
Needle, 2 wooden beads.

Make a small cone

1} Take one of the disks and place it on a flat surface with the pattern side face down. Curl one section of the disk by using the pointed end of a ballpoint pen and create a small cone. Don't curl it too tightly and leave the end open slightly. Use a very small dot of glue to hold the cone in place.

Repeat the process

2} Repeat this on each of the sections on the disk. Once you've done one disk, repeat the process with the remaining seven disks.

Thread the stars together

3} Cut a length of thread, about 50cm (20in) long and tie one bead to the end with a secure knot. Using the needle, make a hole in the centre of one of the stars, pushing the needle through from the patterned side. Now attach another three stars in the same way, but this time, pushing the needle through from the plain side of the star. Push all the stars together to the end of the thread with the bead on.

Add the other stars

4} Take the remaining four stars and attach them onto the thread in the same way as before. This time, thread all of them on from the plain side, the right way up.

Finish assembly

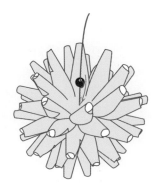

5} Pass the second bead onto the thread and wrap the thread back through the bead so it stays in place on its own. Now push the bead down onto the top star until it stops and the stars form a ball. The bead should stay in place if you've used a thick enough thread and a wooden bead. To stop the star from coming apart, dab a small amount of glue onto the thread where it wraps around the bead.

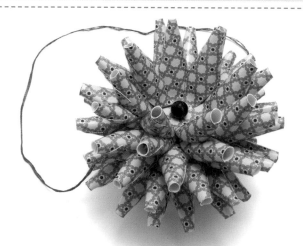

Pointy Star

This highly original paper-star decoration is easy to make and will look beautiful when hung up in your home or create a stir when given as a gift.

Shining
Bright!

Photo Frames

Box Frame

This beautiful box frame would add the finishing touch to the most stylish room. Add a favourite photo to make the perfect gift.

Materials	Skill Level
Card pattern from page 107 1 x C6 Envelope (162x114mm/6x4.5in), A photograph measuring approx. 12.5cmx9cm (5x3.5in)	

Position your photo

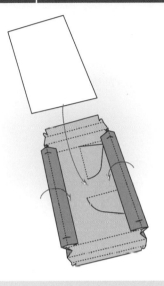

1} Place the frame on a flat surface with the pattern side face down. Place the photograph in the centre of the frame before you start. Now fold the two long sides over to create two square tubes.

Form the ends

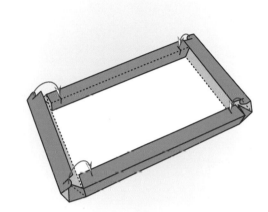

2} Fold over one end and push the little tabs into the slots at the end of each side tube. Repeat with other end.

Stand up

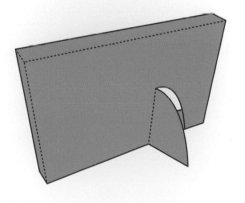

3} Depending whether you have a landscape or portrait photo, fold out one of the stands on the back.

Card pattern from page 107
Glue, Adhesive tack,
five photographs measuring approx. 8cmx8cm (3x3in)

* * * * *

Glue the outer cube

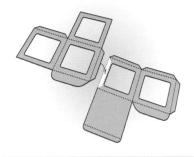

1 } Pre-crease all folds before gluing anything together. Place the outer Cube 1 and outer Cube 2 pieces, pattern side down, on a flat surface in the position shown in the diagram. Glue the two pieces together.

Glue together

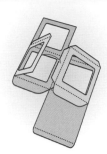

2 } Fold the two outer panels in on each other and glue the tab to the panel.

Make the cube

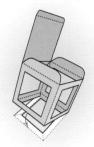

3 } Form this into a cube and fold over the bottom panel. Glue the three glue tabs to the bottom.

Glue together the inner cube

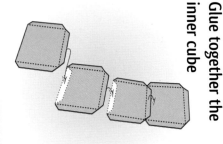

4 } Lay the four inner cube panels in a line as shown in the diagram. Then glue them together as shown.

Form the end panels

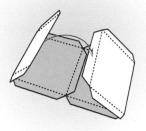

5 } Fold the two end panels in on each other and glue together.

Make a cube

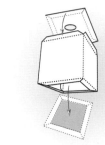

6 } Form the panels into a cube and glue the top and bottom panels to the glue flaps.

7 } Use a small amount of adhesive tack to stick your photos to the sides of the inner cube. Then slide the inner cube into the outer cube and close the lid.

Attach your photos

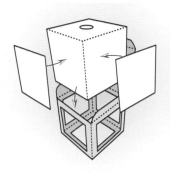

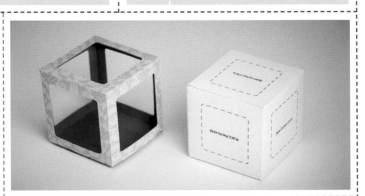

Memories!

Photo Cube

A great way to display up to five pictures in one place. Turn the cube around to change what is on view.

Polaroid Photo Frame

This easy-to-make frame will transform a simple photo into something that you can display with pride.

Photographer at Work!

Attach the strengthener

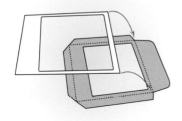

1 } Pre-crease all folds. Lay the front piece on a flat surface with the black side facing up. Using a small amount of glue, attach the strengthener as shown.

Glue on the back

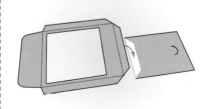

2 } Attach the frame to the back carefully lining up the glue tab with the white glue area.

Fold over the glue flaps

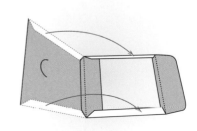

3 } Fold over the two side glue flaps on the front piece, then fold over the back piece and glue in place.

Glue on the strut

4 } Glue the strut in place onto the back piece. Insert your photo.

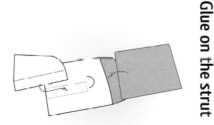

Fold out and tuck in

5 } Fold out the stand to 90 degrees. Fold over the top flap and tuck it into the little half moon tab on the back.

Materials	Skill Level
Card pattern from page 115 Glue, Adhesive tack, A photo measuring approx. 90x50cm (35x20in)	

Bon
Voyage!

Luggage Style Tag

This fun project makes a one-off photo frame that you can attach to anything you like or use as a gift tag.

Attach the strengthener

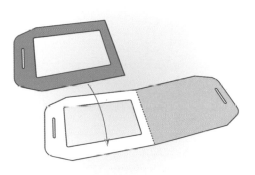

1 } Pre-crease all folds. Lay the tag on a flat surface with the white panel face up. Glue the strengthener to the white glue panel area.

Add a photo

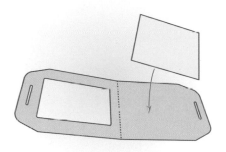

2 } Take your photograph and use a small amount of adhesive tack to hold it in place.

Wrap around

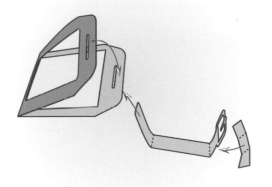

3 } Fold over the tag and push the strap through the slots. Then wrap the band around the strap at the buckle end and secure with a small amount of glue.

Finish assembly

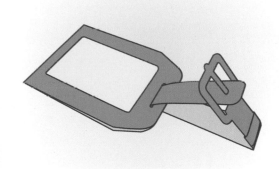

4 } Finally, push the end of the strap through the buckle and then into the band to secure it.

Boxes

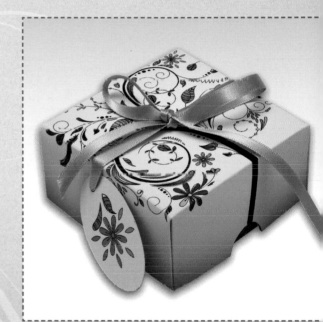

Materials	Skill Level
Card pattern from page 117 Glue, two lengths of fabric ribbon approx. 25cm (10in) long and 35cm (14in) long	✳ ✳ ✳ ✳ ✳

Glue the two sections

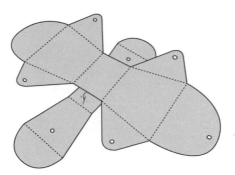

1} Pre-crease all folds before gluing anything together. Place the two halves of the box across each other at right angles on a flat surface with the pattern side face down. Glue the central rectangles together.

Fold up the sides

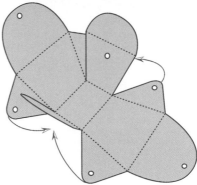

2} Fold up the four sides and then fold round the four side flaps so they overlap each other and the holes line up. Fix the sides in place with a small dot of glue.

Add ribbon to assemble

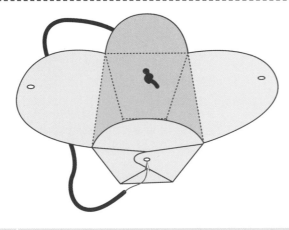

3} Take the shorter length of ribbon and push one end through the holes in one end of the box. Now tie several knots to make one large knot making sure it is big enough so as not to pull through the hole. Take the other end and push it through the hole in the opposite end of the box. Tie knots in this end, again making sure it won't pull through the hole. Finish by using the longer length of ribbon to tie the two top flaps together.

Fancy Box

An exquisite box to make that will be an object of admiration however you decide to use it.

Milk Carton Style Box

This quirky design can be used to gift wrap special items with style and will really impress your friends!

Materials	Skill Level

Card pattern from page 121
Glue, length of fabric ribbon approx. 25cm (10in) long

Glue the two halves

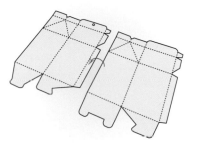

1} Pre-crease all folds before gluing anything together. Lay the two sides on a flat surface in the positions shown. Then glue the two halves together.

Fold and glue panels

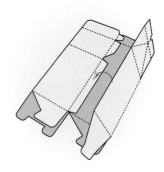

2} Turn the box over and fold the two outer panels inwards, to meet each other. Glue the tab to the panel.

Fold over the lid flaps

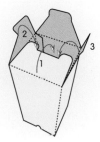

3} Stand the box on its end with the shaped flaps facing upwards. Now carefully push the box into a square tube shape. Fold over Flap 1 first. Then fold over Flaps 2 and 3 and tuck the little curved ends under Flap 1.

Finish the box

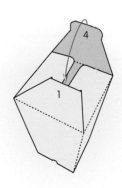

4} Close the end by folding over flap 4 and tucking it inside flap 1. Now turn the box the right way up.

Tie the ribbon round

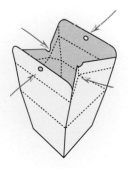

5} Push the sides inwards until the two flaps with the holes meet each other. Finish by securing the top with the ribbon.

Materials	Skill Level

Card pattern from page 129
Glue, Fabric ribbon approx. 60cm (24in) long

✱ ✱ ✱ ✱ ✱

Add the front and side panels

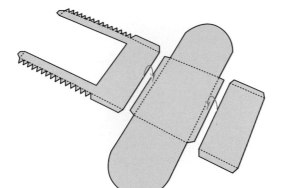

1} Pre-crease all folds before gluing anything together. Place the sides, front and back on a flat surface with the pattern side face down. Arrange them in the position shown and then glue the two tabs on the side panel to the front and back.

Glue the ends up

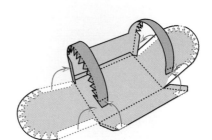

2} Fold up the front panel and glue the two ends of the back panel in place. Put a small dot of glue on each of the little triangular tabs and on the two long tabs. Carefully fold up one side at a time and attach the glue tabs, making sure each triangle is stuck down.

Finish and tie with a ribbon

3} Glue the lid to the back of the box. Now attach the ribbon and wrap it around the box, tying it in a bow at the front to hold the lid closed.

Treasure Chest Style Box

This pretty little chest will hold your most treasured possessions. Make it for a friend or keep it for yourself!

Little Goodies!

Lift-off Lid Box

Make this simple box and use it in so many different ways from storing your jewellery or packing up a special gift.

Card pattern from page 125
Glue,
Fabric ribbon approx. 50cm (20in) long

Fold up two sides and the top

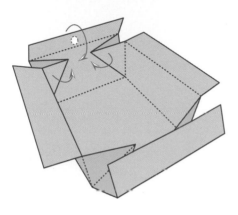

1} Pre-crease all folds before gluing anything together. Lay the base on a flat surface with the pattern side face down. Fold up one side, pushing the two corners inwards to make a 'V' shape. Now fold over the top flap and hold in place with a small dot of glue. Repeat on the opposite side.

Fold up the other two sides

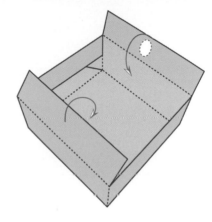

2} Fold over the two remaining sides and hold in place with a small dot of glue.

Finish with a ribbon

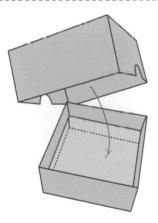

3} Repeat steps 1 and 2 for the lid. Slide the base inside the lid and finish with the ribbon.

Party

Celebrate in Style!

Bunting

Bunting is fun and friendly and can be used on many different occasions, from parties to weddings and fairs. Using your own ribbons and threads will make your bunting unique. Be inventive!

Cut your ribbon

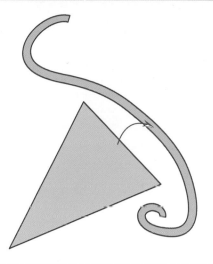

1} Cut the ribbon to the required length, depending on how much bunting you want to make. Allow about 10cm (4in) between each paper flag.

Glue or stitch

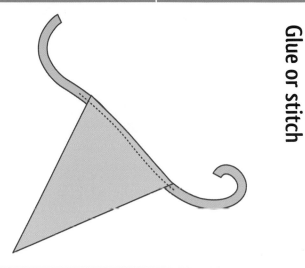

2} For a quick way of making bunting, just use a small amount of glue to attach each flag to the ribbon. For a more permanent way of making your bunting, either use a needle and thread or a sewing machine to attach each flag. You could use a contrasting coloured thread for an even bigger impact.

Materials	Skill Level
Card pattern from page 135 Glue, Double-sided sticky foam pads, Scissors	

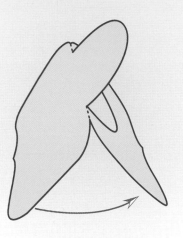

Fold and add a name

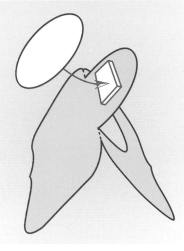

Make them stand out

1} Pre-crease all folds. To make a standard place card, fold the card in half and stand upright. Write the person's name in the banner area.

2} Alternatively, you can use the matching 'Invite Add-on' to create a 3-D effect. Take a foam pad and use this to create the relief.

Perfect Party!

Place Cards

Make your guests feel very special by placing these around the table when they come round for a meal.

Come Dine
with me!

Napkin Rings

Why not make an everyday meal a little more special by putting these pretty napkin rings on the table?

Materials	Skill Level
Card pattern from page 139 Glue	* * * * *

Very gently curl each napkin ring over the edge of a table until the card forms a full circle. Be careful not the crease or dent the card. Now glue the ends together making sure the glue has completely dried before using them.

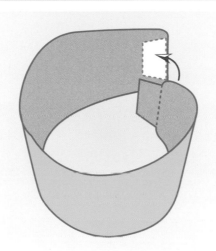

Curl round

Materials	Skill Level
Card pattern from page 141 Glue, Double-sided sticky foam pads, Scissors, Card, Envelopes, Craft knife	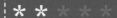

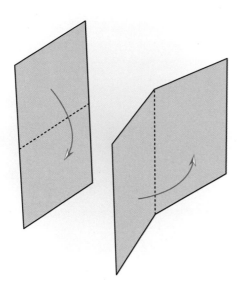

1⟩ Choose a coloured or patterned card that fits well with the invite add-ons you would like to use. You will also need envelopes, so cut the card to a size that's twice the size of your envelope and then fold in half. If you use thick card, you may find it easier to gently score the card with the back of a craft knife.

2⟩ Cut a foam pad into small squares and use these to create layers with the add-ons. You can use several layers to make more of a 3-D effect.

Party On!

Invite Add-ons

These beautiful designs can be made in three-dimensional objects using sticky foam pads and then stuck on to your party invites for a truly original effect.

SIDE

ROOF

SIDE

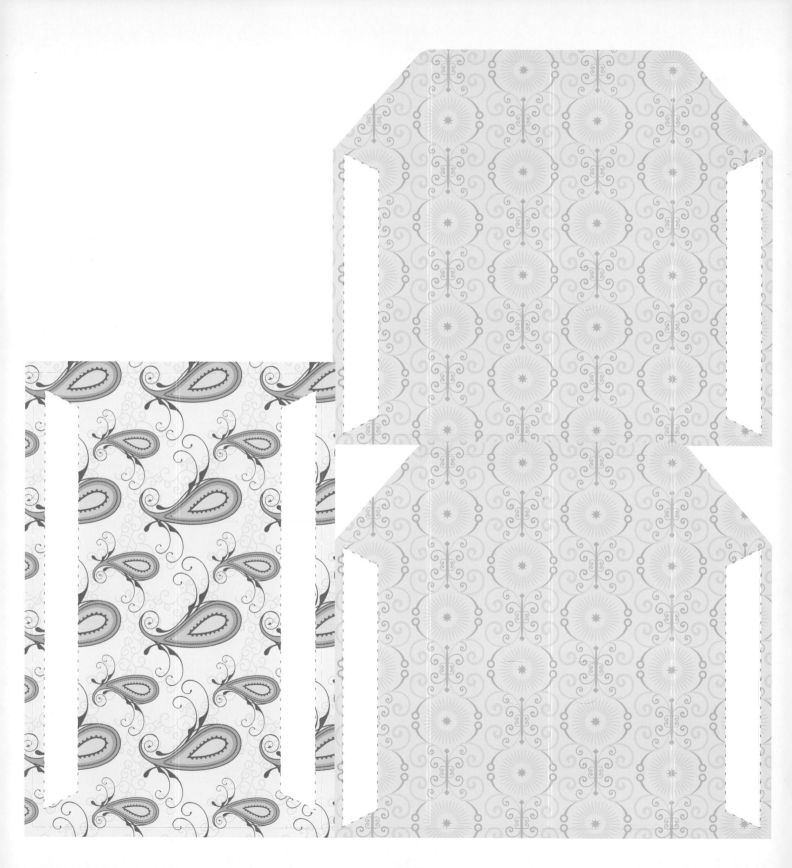

CARD

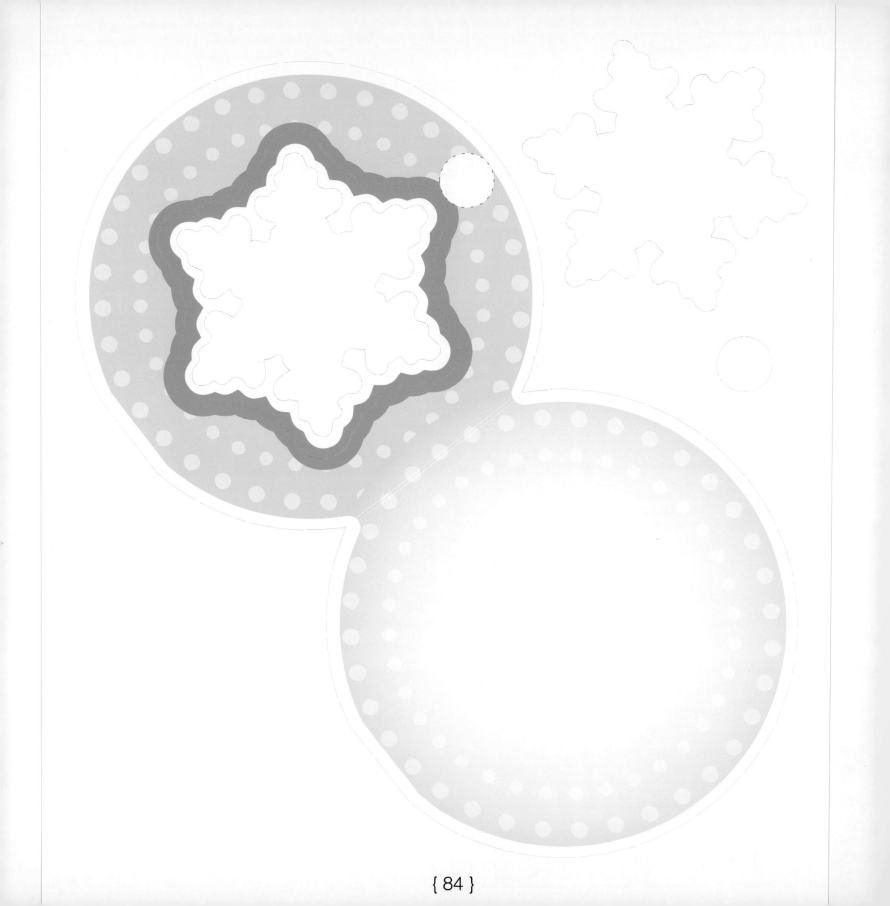

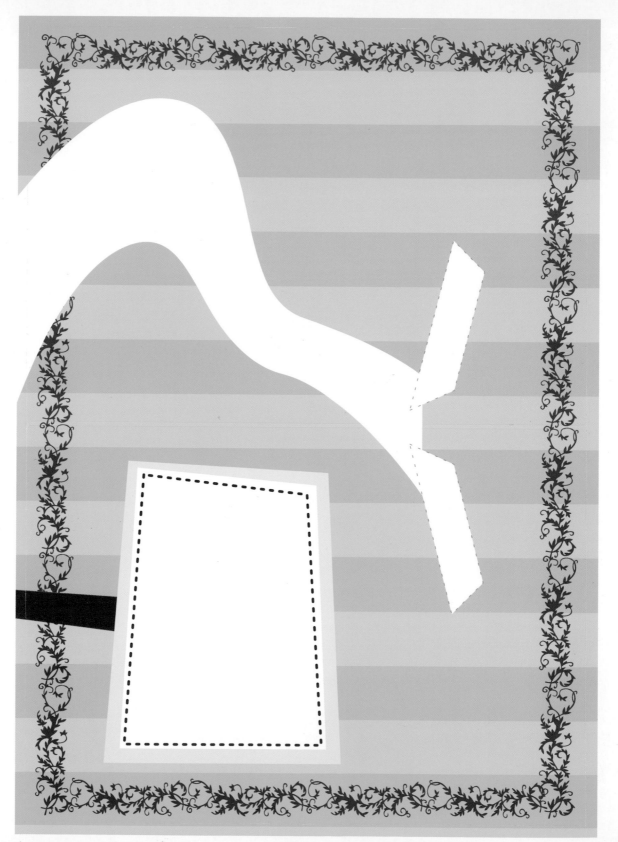

HEART

HOUSE

BACKGROUND LAYER 1

BACKGROUND LAYER 2

MINI HOUSE

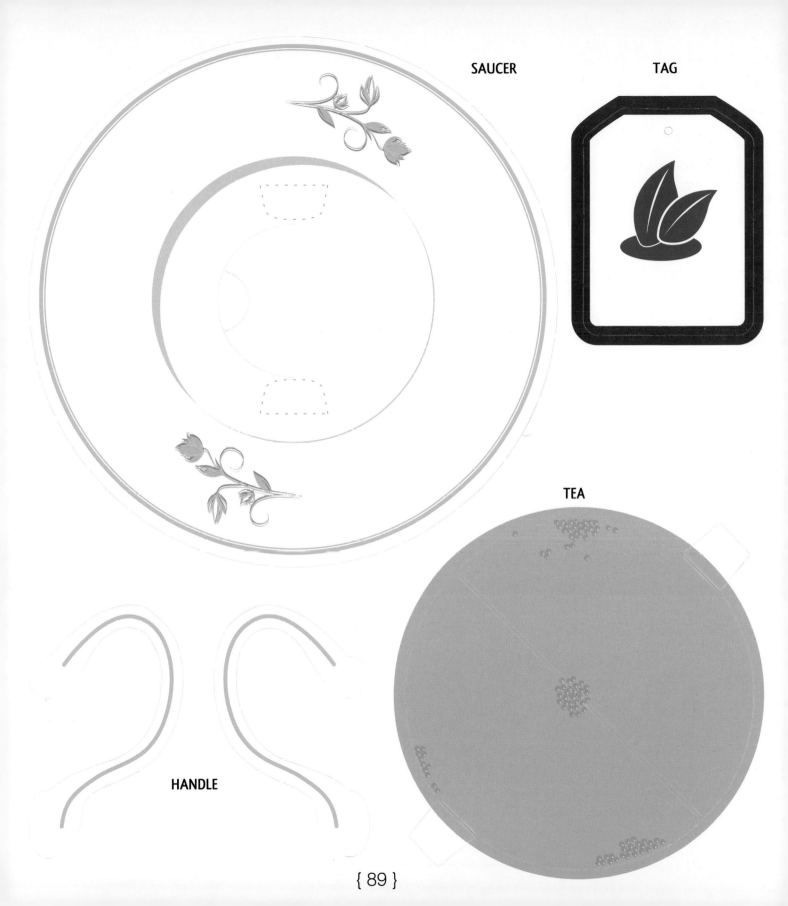

SAUCER

TAG

TEA

HANDLE

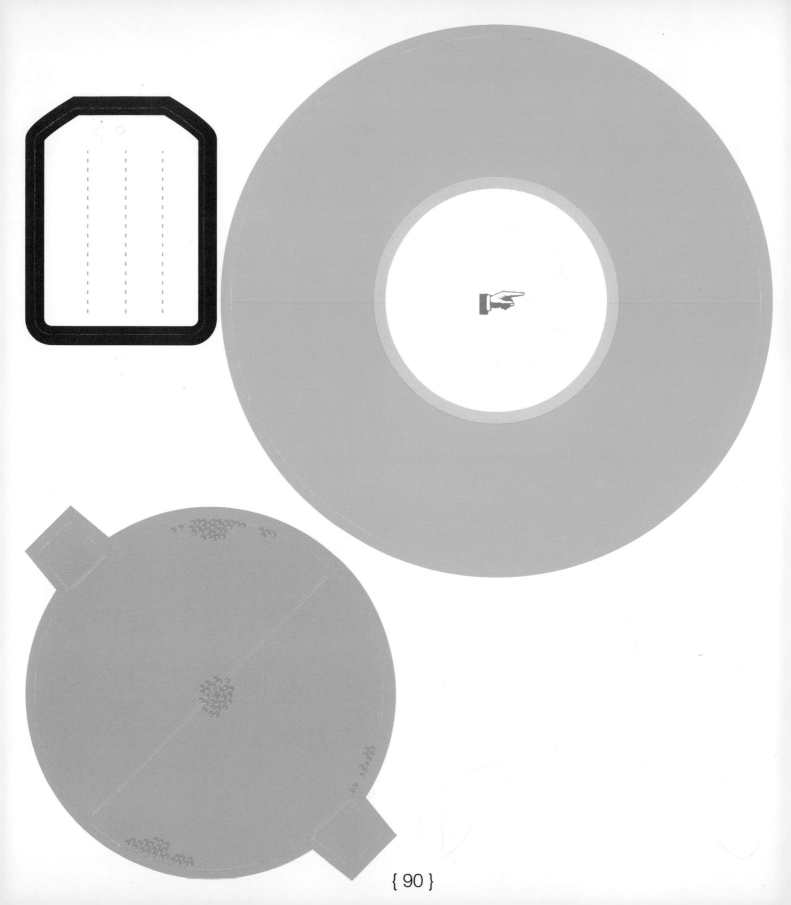

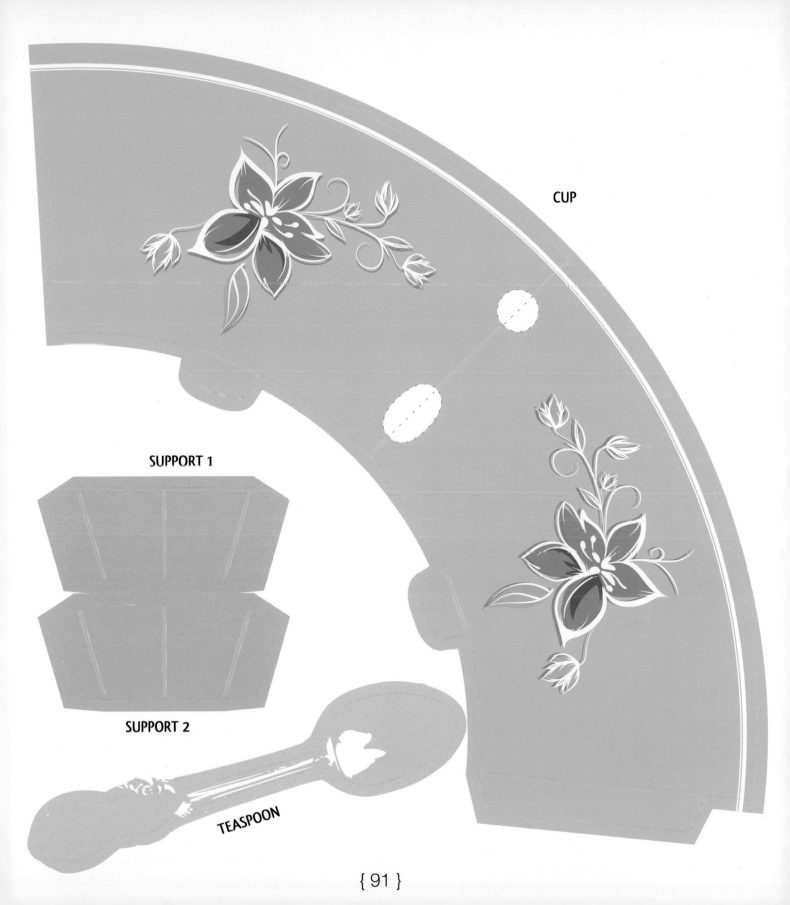

CUP

SUPPORT 1

SUPPORT 2

TEASPOON

{ 91 }

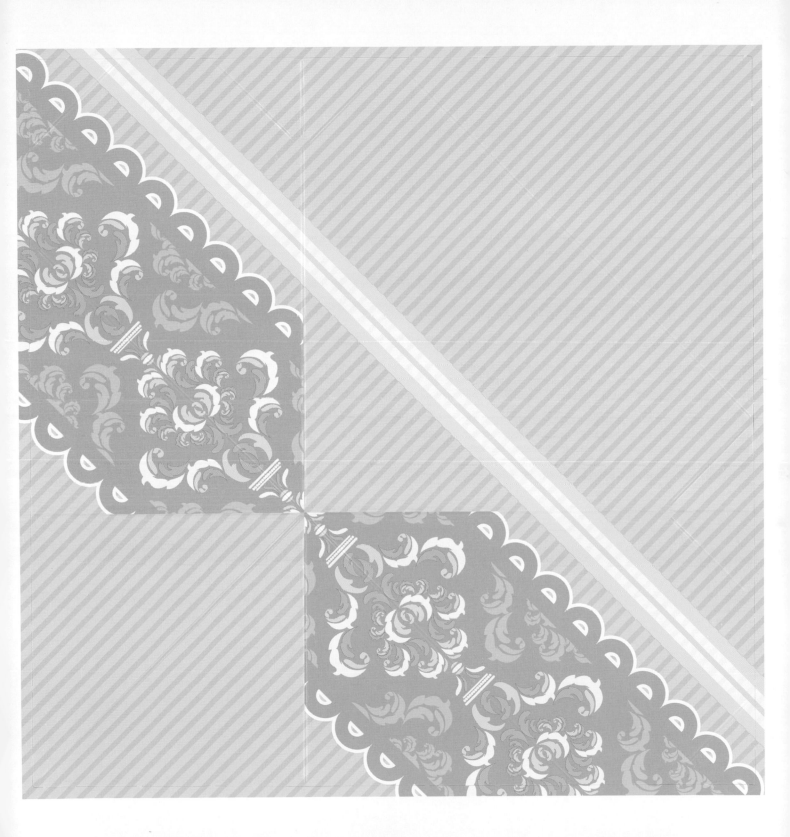

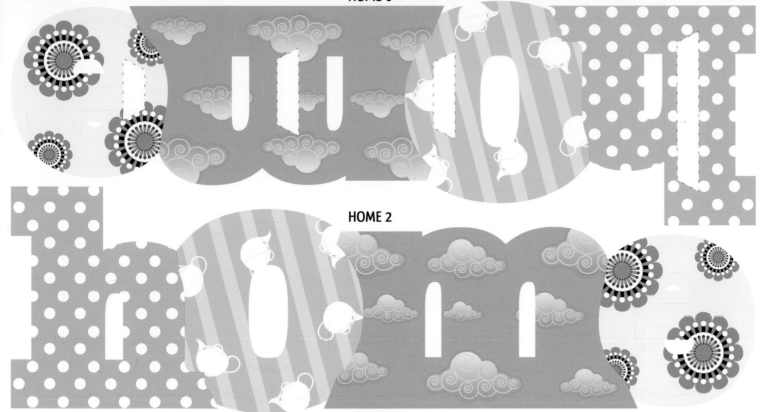

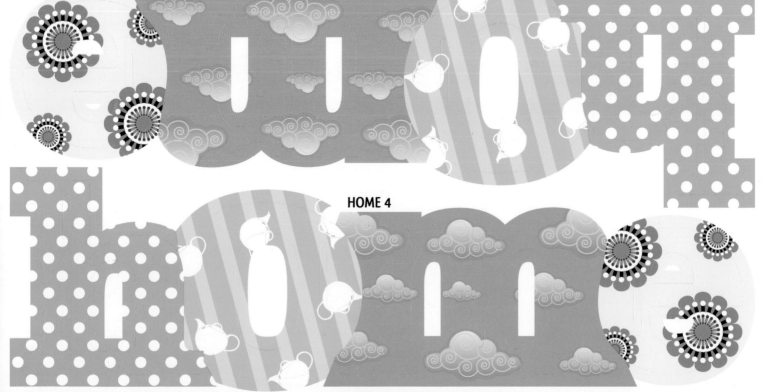

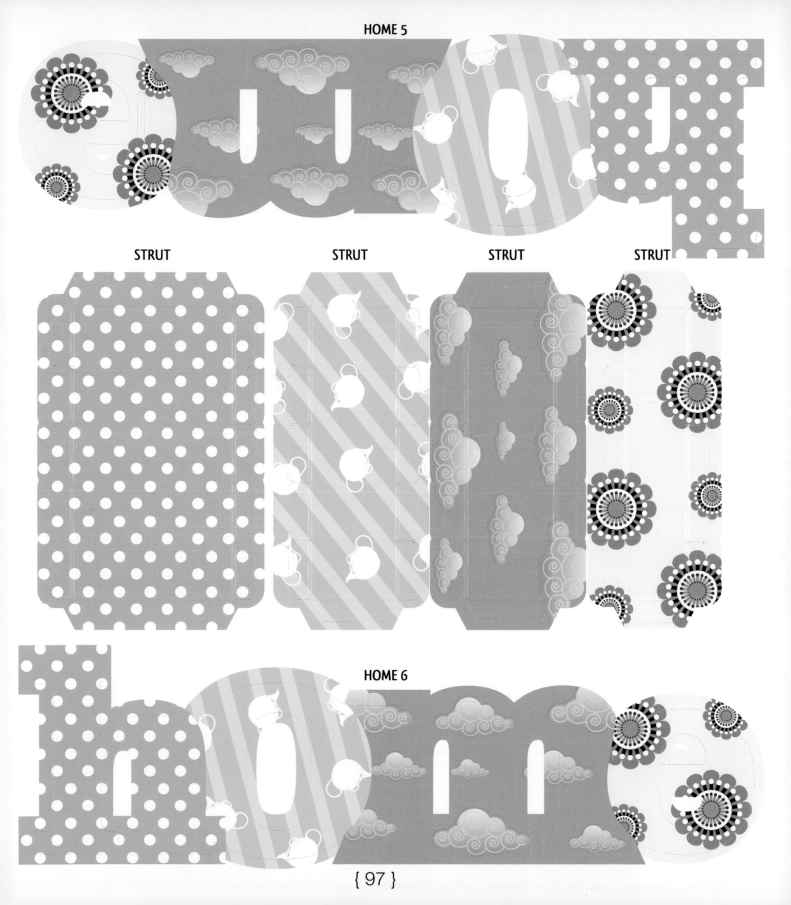

STRUT STRUT STRUT STRUT

HOME 6

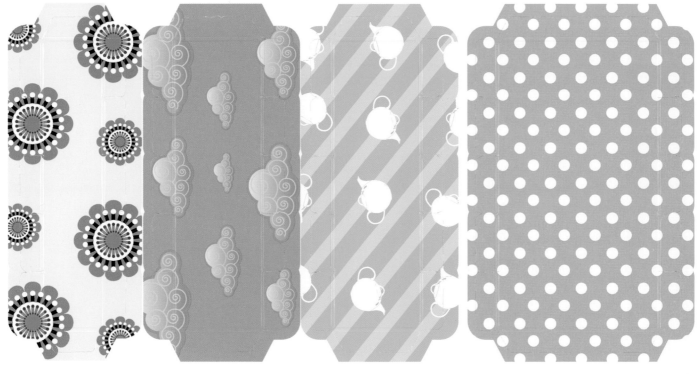

BIRD BACK

INSIDE LEG

TOP

BIRD FRONT

INSIDE LEG

BASE

PIVOT

LEGS

{ 99 }

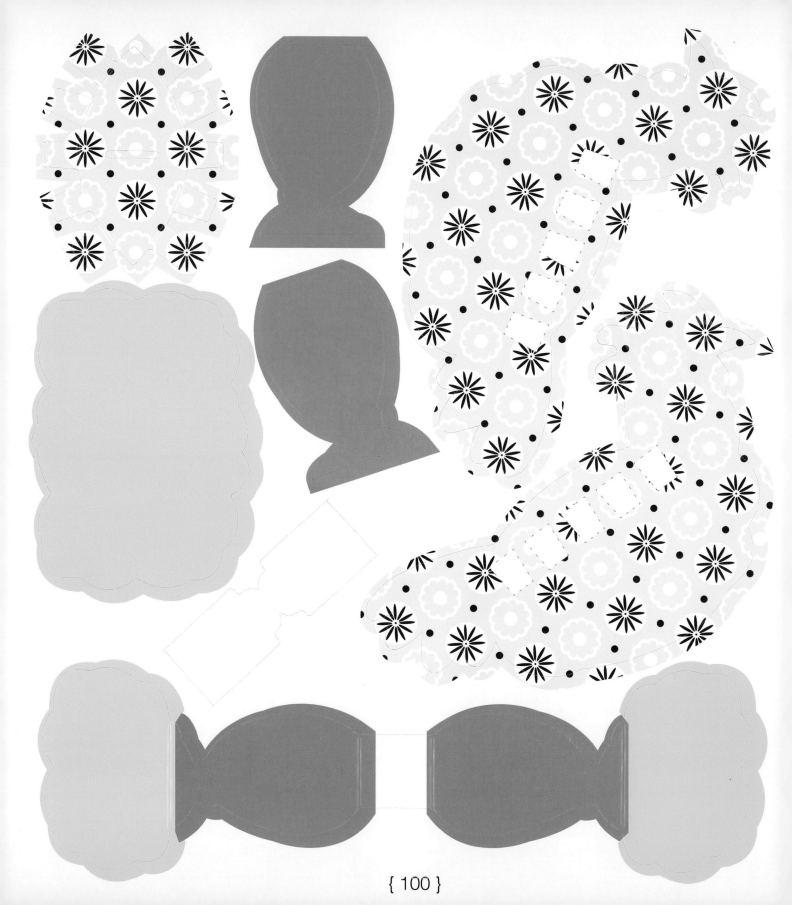

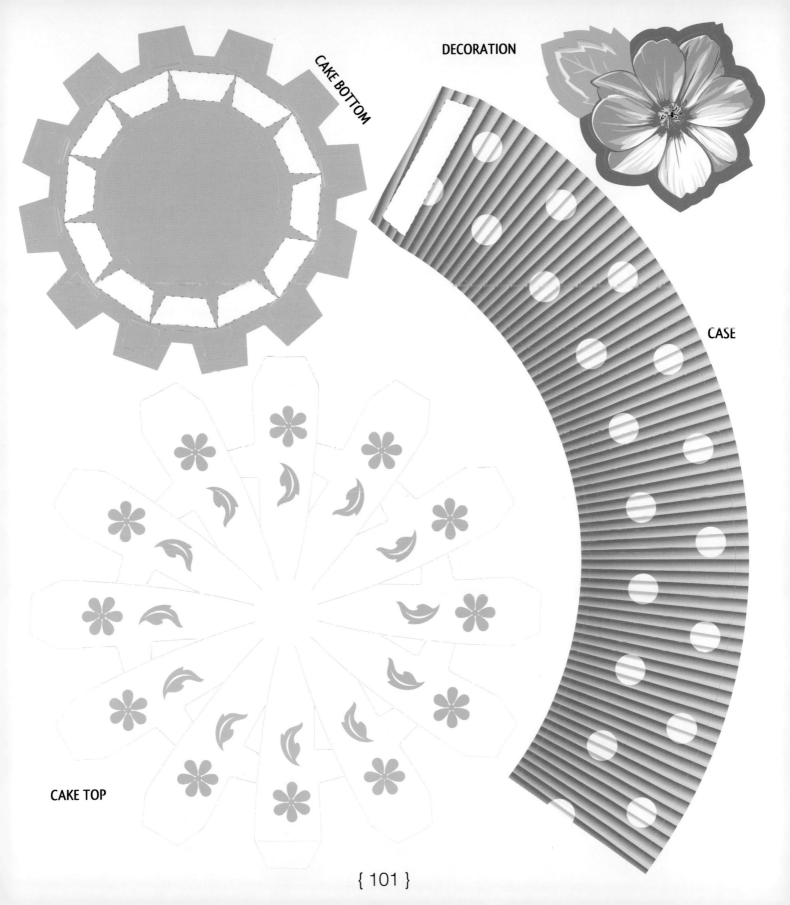

CAKE BOTTOM

DECORATION

CASE

CAKE TOP

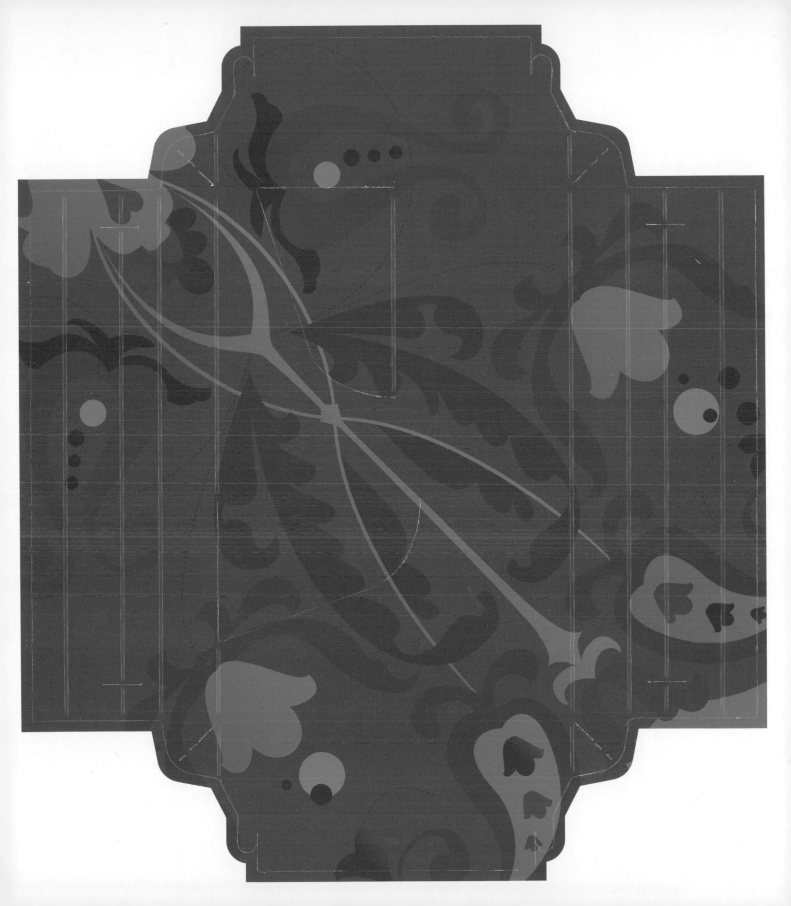

OUTER CUBE 1

INNER CUBE BOTTOM

PULL HERE

PULL HERE

{ 109 }

OUTER CUBE 2

INNER CUBE TOP

PLACE PHOTO HERE

INNER CUBE SIDE 1

INNER CUBE SIDE 2

PLACE PHOTO HERE

PLACE PHOTO HERE

PLACE PHOTO HERE

PLACE PHOTO HERE

INNER CUBE SIDE 3

INNER CUBE SIDE 4

STAND

FRONT

BACK

STRENGTHENER

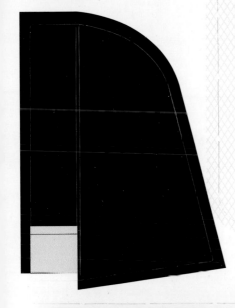

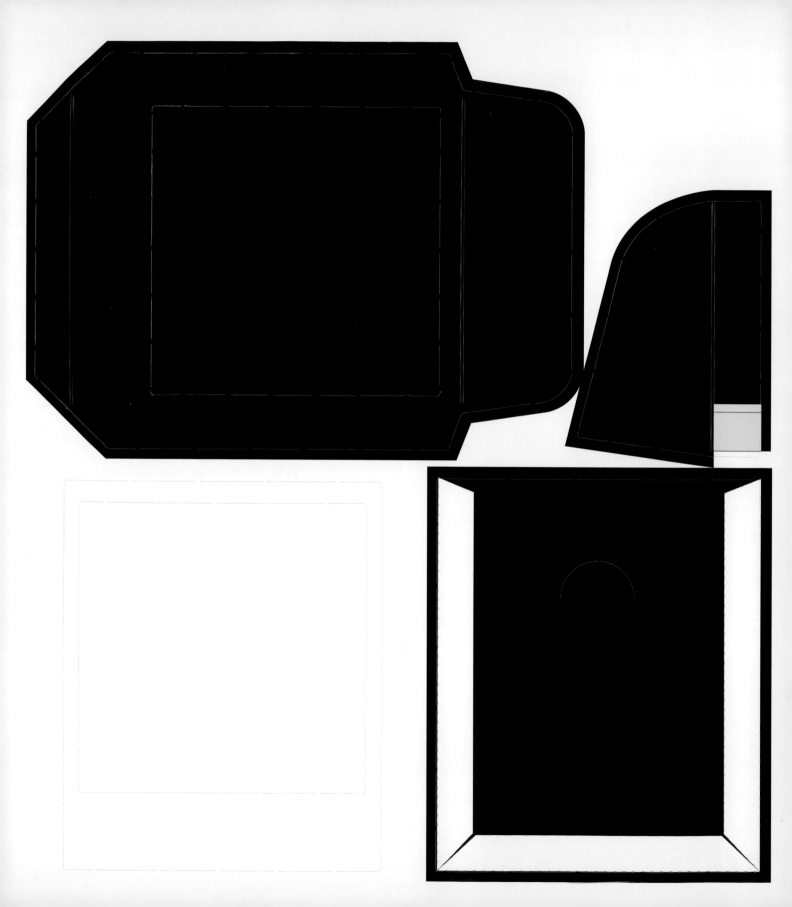

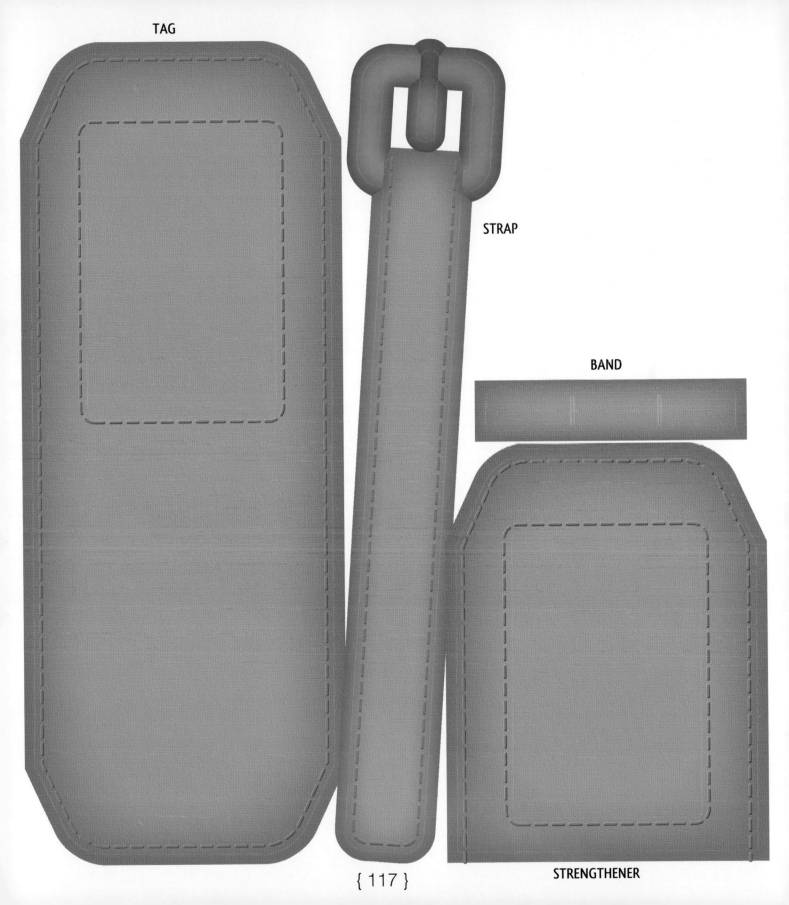

TAG

STRAP

BAND

STRENGTHENER

PANEL 1

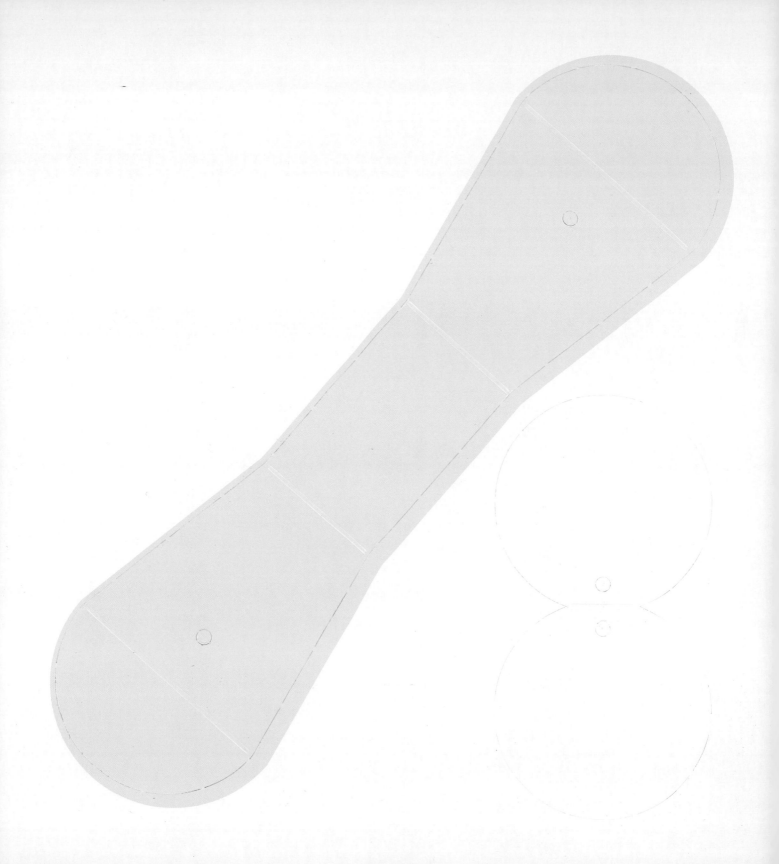

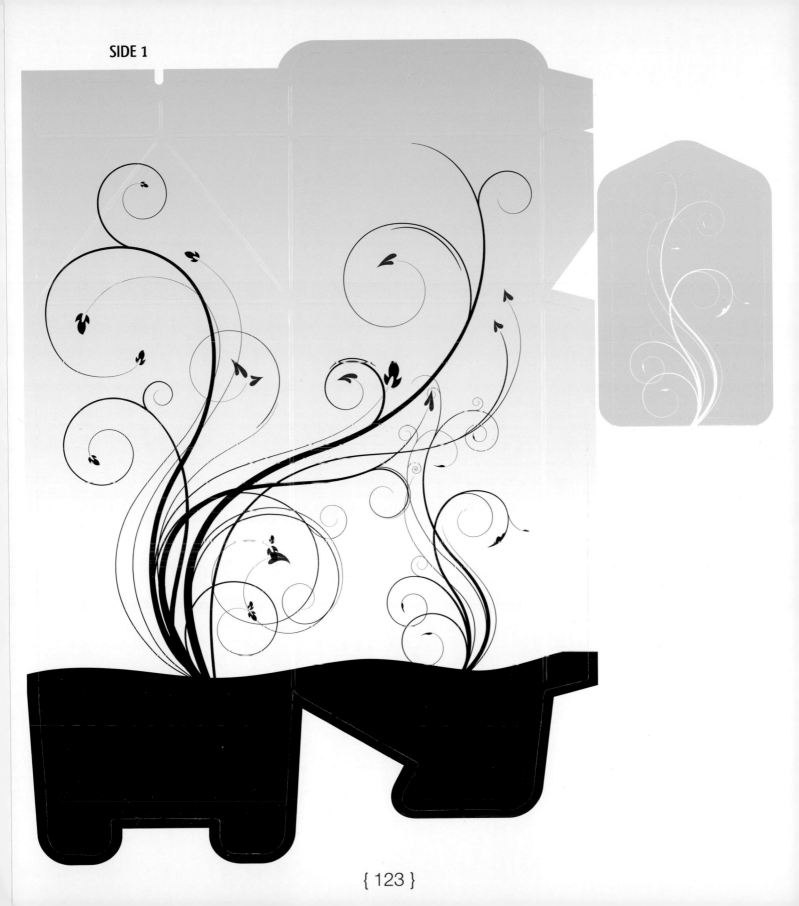

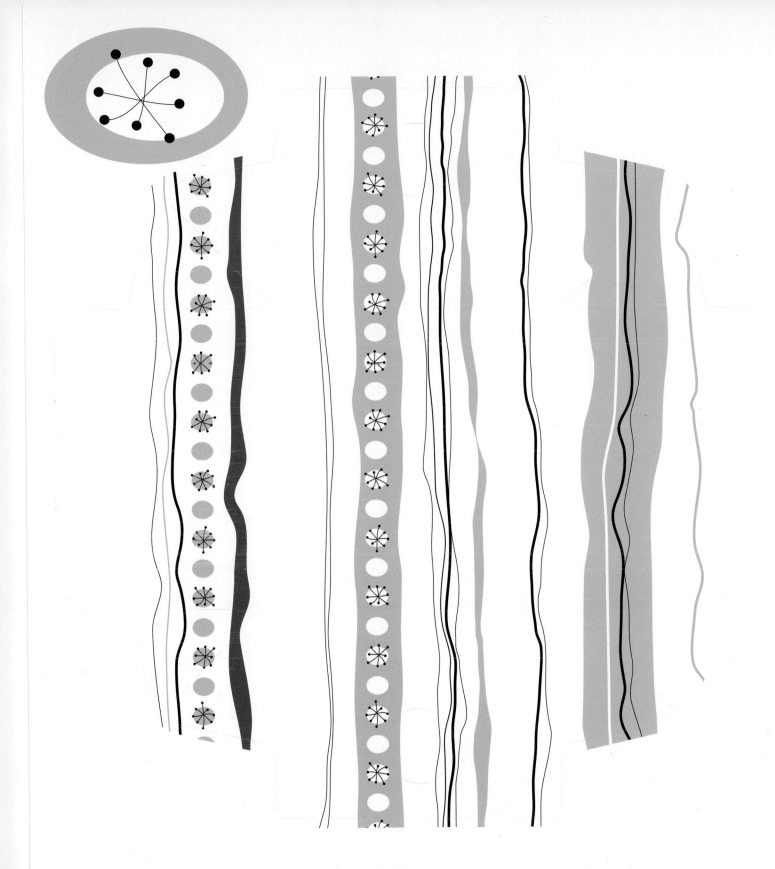

SIDES

LID

FRONT

BACK

{ 131 }

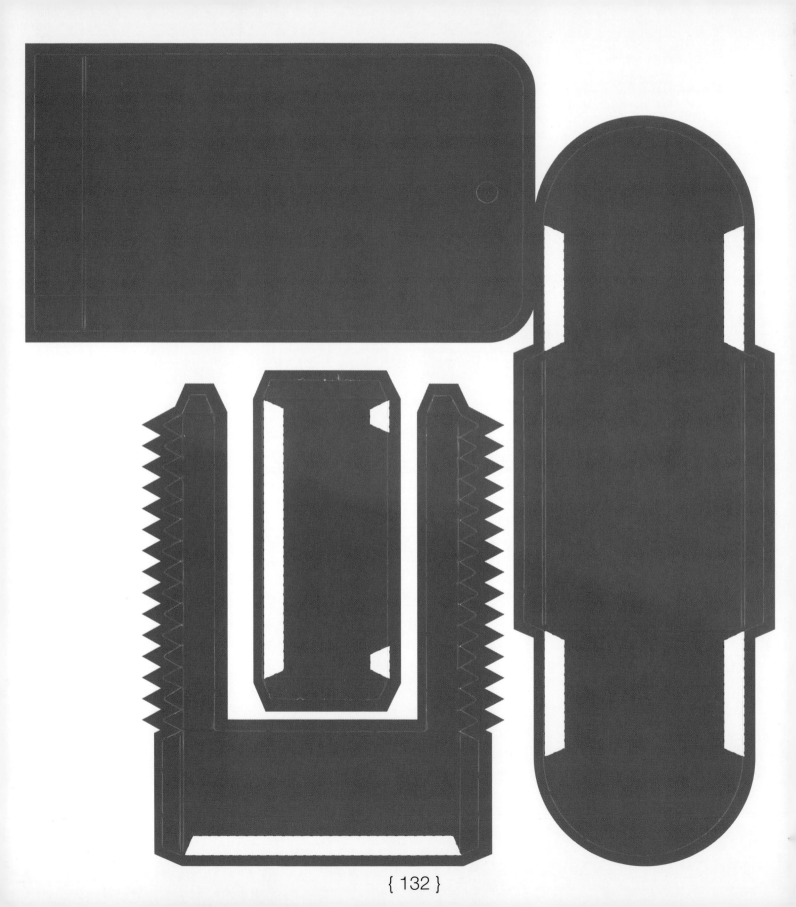

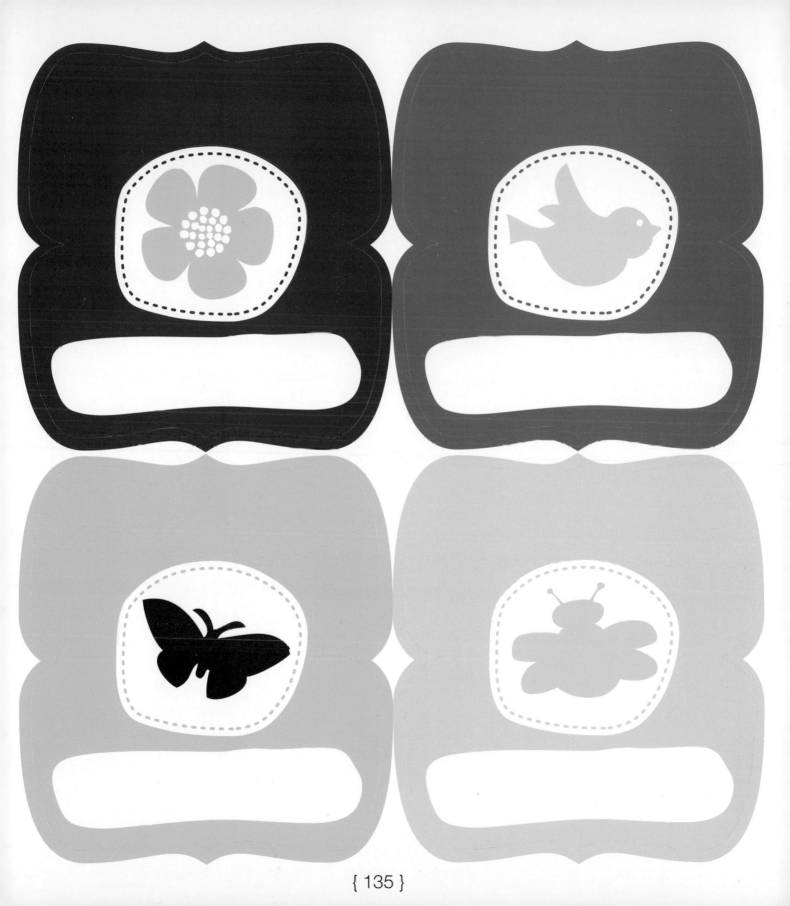

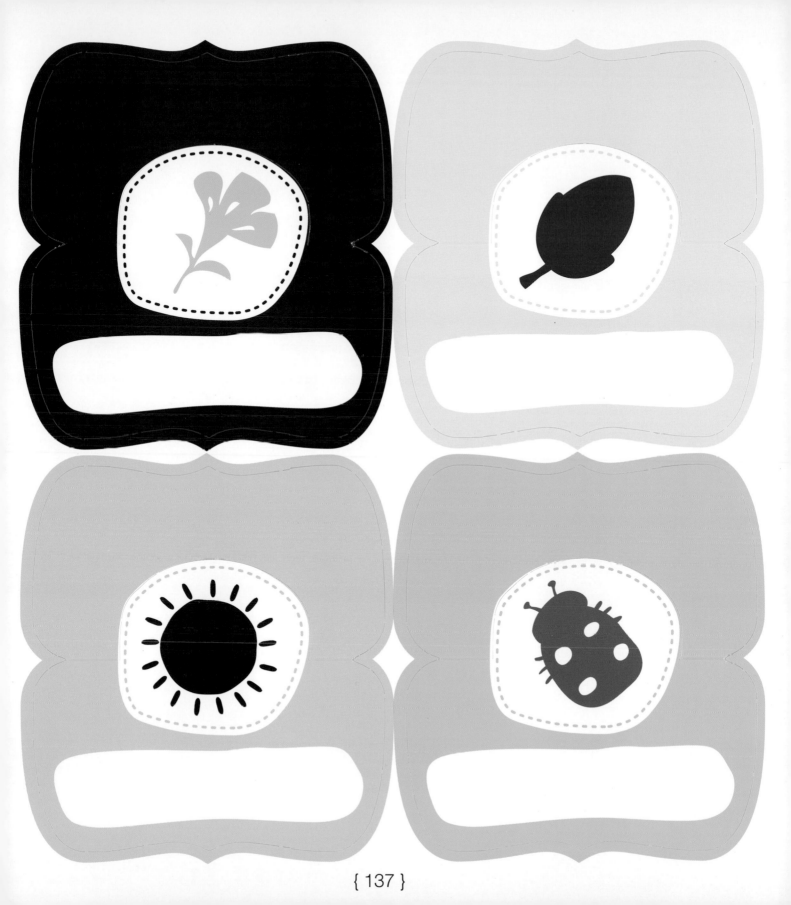

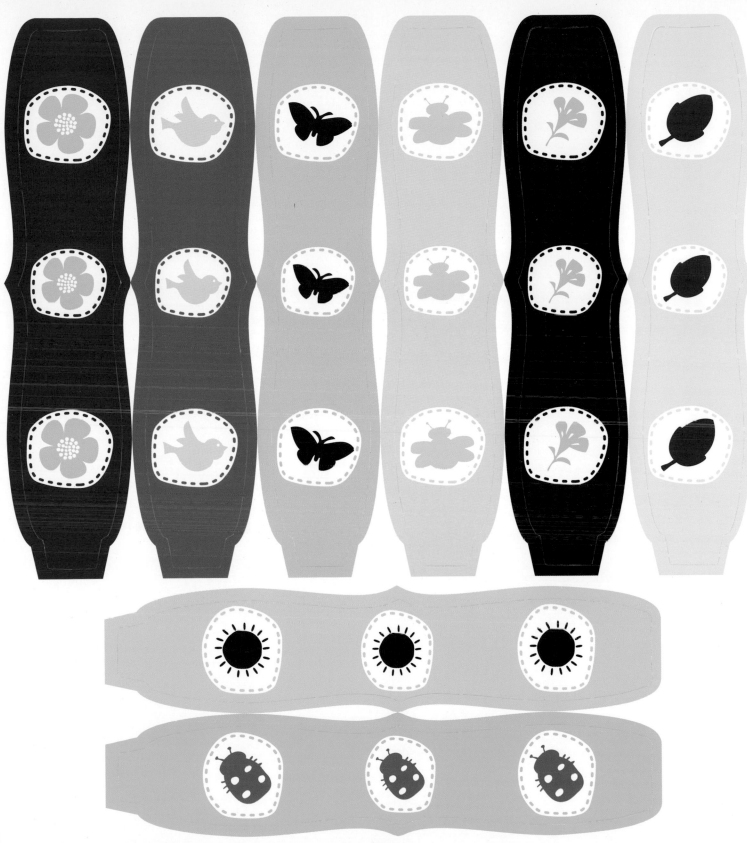